Something is
Missing...
I Want
More!

Something is Missing... I Want More!

A Single Mom's Guide to Finding Her Path

Sharita Latham

Something is Missing... I Want More! A Single Mom's Guide to Finding Her Path

by Sharita Latham

© Copyright 2018, SHARITA LATHAM. All rights reserved.

No part of this publication may be reproduced, stored in a retrieval system, or transmitted in any form or by any means, electronic, mechanical, photocopying, recording, or otherwise, without the prior permission of the copyright owner, except for brief quotations included in a review of the book.

ISBN-13: 978-0-692-16042-8

Printed in the U.S.A.

To my mother who has been my support system and example.

To my son, Isaiah, whom I love and cherish.

And to every woman who has ever been a single mom. This is for you.

Contents

Introduction..9

Chapter 1: Desire...........................…..................13
- ❖ My Desire, My Path
- ❖ Listen! Listen to Your Instincts!

Chapter 2: Discovery............……................21
- ❖ What is the Root?
- ❖ My Discovery, My Path
- ❖ Enlightened
- ❖ Don't Tell Everybody
- ❖ What About the Children?
- ❖ My Son

Chapter 3: Decision..................…..............42
- ❖ Looking Back, It Hurt Me More Than I Knew
- ❖ My Decision, My Path
- ❖ Get Your Mind Right, It May Not Get Easier
- ❖ They Might Support You, They Might Not
- ❖ I Decided and Leaped
- ❖ What About the Children?

- ❖ A Whole Lot Changed, and Some Things Stayed the Same

Chapter 4: What We Want……………………..68

Chapter 5: From My Heart to Yours
Principles to Live By……………………………...72

Chapter 6: Self-Examination…………………..84
- ❖ Being a Single Mom
- ❖ Triggers
- ❖ Expectations

Chapter 7: Your Love Life………………....……94
- ❖ Yes, a Man Will Love You and Your Children

Chapter 8: Words Have Power
Words of Affirmation………………………...102
- ❖ Words of Encouragement to Single Moms from Supporters Around the World

A Special Thank You to My Supporters……..111

About the Author…………………………..113

Introduction

I wrote this book for all the single moms who feel as if something is missing in their life. You may feel a sense of urgency to make a change and start over with your children, but you are not sure why or what that means. Sometimes we settle and have children before we really know what else life has to offer. Although you may have created a lifestyle that is familiar, maybe there is a better life waiting. Finding the path meant for you is your gateway to *having more.* Listen to your heart; it knows when something is missing. Leaving everything behind and transitioning into something new can be a scary process, but you can do it. I promise!

The first step to finding your path begins within your mind. In this book, I will discuss the 3 D's—Desire, Discovery, and Decision—which will guide you towards what is missing and how to get more. They do not always happen in this order; they didn't for me. Finding the path *to more* is a process that will happen differently depending on where you are in life. Use this book as a guide. You must start somewhere, or you'll look back ten years later and be in the exact same place.

Growing up as a child, I was a dreamer, I was a believer, and I could not imagine a world where my dreams no longer seemed possible. Then I grew up, life happened, and I became a mom. Holding my son in my arms didn't make me remember my dreams, it made me realize how much I love him and how much I would do whatever it takes to make sure he was taken care of. That is exactly what I did; I followed a path that ensured his wellbeing. Honorable, right?

Absolutely! So why didn't I feel 100% sure that I was doing everything that I could for him? It took me a few years, but I finally figured it out. I have learned that although I am a single mom, I am a woman first. I needed to transition my mind, to transition my life so I could show my son what is possible. I now understand how important it is for me to find my path as a woman, so I could be the best mom.

As you read this book, take your time. Allow it to be your own personal journal. Throughout the book, I have provided questions for you to answer as you take this journey. Answer them honestly, even if the answers are not positive. Knowing how you truly feel and think, allows you to know what changes you need to make.

Chapter 1

Desire

Desire is internal. It is a deep longing for something that you may or may not initially understand. The desire *for more* is different for every mom. It can start with wanting a career change, wanting to challenge yourself in new ways, wanting to give your family a better life, or wanting to leave an environment that is emotionally, mentally, or physically harmful. It can start with feeling dissatisfied or simply having questions about what else you can do with your life.

Take time to search out your desires and the reasons behind them. If you do not know why you *want more* or what exactly you want, that's okay; I'm here to guide you towards figuring it out.

As you move forward, be sure to pray for clarity. Often, our doubts and fears cloud our minds and become a hindrance. If you have noticed a longing inside and have just ignored it or convinced yourself that it is nothing, stop that immediately. Even if it is just a small longing that keeps coming back, it is okay. That small prompting can grow into something you never imagined if you let it.

1. What do you desire?

Chapter 1: Desire

2. When did you first notice this desire?

3. Why do you believe you have this desire?

Chapter 1: Desire

My Desire, My Path

I was born and raised in a small city in Indiana. Everything I knew revolved around this one location. I went to school there all the way through college, lived with my mom, rented a house, bought a house, had the same job for almost eight years, knew the same group of people, and had my son, all in the same city. Everyone knew everyone and nothing new was ever happening. When I began to examine my life and everything that I had already accomplished, I was not satisfied. ***Something was missing.***

I had such a limited perspective of the world and what was even possible that I didn't know what I could do or who I could be. I did not know how to be anyone other than the woman who felt limited, and that was not enough! Sure, graduating from college with my bachelor's degree, buying a house at twenty-four, having a good paying job, and taking care of my son are great accomplishments—but, still, not enough. I needed to figure out what else was missing, what else I needed, and where this desire **for more** came from.

I had more questions than answers. Frustration caused me to just want to give up—and I tried to, a few times. I even tried to convince myself that I was just being ungrateful, that nothing was wrong, that it was all in my head, that maybe I was just bored. But God allowed the desire for *more* to keep growing and growing. I am thankful that He did not give up on me even when I wanted to give up on myself.

Chapter 1: Desire

Listen! Listen to Your Instincts!

Maybe you have traveled the world and had a lot of diverse experiences. Or, maybe, like me, you come from a small city, and still can't shake the feeling that something is missing. Based on my experiences, I believe our instincts guide our desires; they are a God-given compass meant to lead us towards what's next. That is something to be excited about because it means that there is a whole new life, a whole new adventure, just waiting for you to arrive.

Nothing has to be wrong for you to have this unshakeable desire. Maybe you were just hired for the job you always wanted, bought a new house, purchased a new car, or accomplished a long-pursued goal. But, inside, something is *still missing*. And, maybe, the path you are on now is not where you are meant to be. Once the excitement wears off, if you are not on the right path,

Chapter 1: Desire

your true desires will keep you wanting more.

Chapter 2

Discovery

What is the Root?

The root of our desires can go all the way back to childhood. They can go back to a defining moment in your life where you discovered something that brought you **internal joy, expressed passion**, and a **confirmation in your soul,** where you said, **"This Is It!"** That desire is something that only you may understand. If you have not found that yet, that's okay. The simple fact that you have the desire is a sign that there is more to be discovered.

Don't dismiss anything in your life that gave you that **"This Is It!"** feeling, regardless of the outcome. Just because things do not go as planned or have an unfavorable outcome does not mean that it is something that is not meant to be a part of you. Maybe you lost a competition, didn't get the promotion, failed a class, embarrassed yourself, or had someone tell you that you can't. None of those things matter. What's on the inside will tell you more than anything on the outside. You can always get better, you can always try again, and there will be other people who believe that you can.

Discovering the root of your desires should be fun. Forget everything else going on and write down what you want, what you would like to try, what you have already done and enjoyed doing, and what those things mean for your life. Does it mean new opportunities? Traveling more? New friends? A career change? More money? Right now, your answer may be very broad; there's nothing wrong with that. Do not be afraid to write down and say aloud exactly what you want! Do not think of the obstacles, what others might think, or all the reasons why you can't. Right now, anything is possible.

1. Have you ever had a "This Is It!" moment? Describe your "This Is It!" moment(s).

2. Describe how those moments made you feel.

3. What activities can you get involved in that will allow you to start doing what you enjoy again?

4. What new path do you need to take based on your discovery?

My Discovery, My Path

To my surprise, after years of working in the corporate world and being exhausted by the long hours and high demands, I was laid off. At that moment, I faced my greatest fear: no money, and no control over what happened. I no longer felt secure. The possibility of being unemployed was the main reason I never took chances. I never wanted to be put in that position. I had nothing but time and I had no plan. In my subconscious, I had hopes and dreams, but my first instinct was to find another job immediately. However, before I could do that, I spent the day at the beach with a woman named Angela Sims who became my coach soon after I was laid off. I sat and talked with her about being laid off and she helped me understand that the time I had been given was a gift. I could focus on all the other things I wanted to do, but I wasn't sure what those things were.

Chapter 2: Discovery

We took a journey down memory lane to discover all the things I was passionate about. I wrote down the things that gave me **internal joy, expressed passion,** and a **confirmation in my soul.** I found that I was doing everything but the things I loved. I enjoyed creative writing, songwriting, plays, and singing, and I had a journal full of movie concepts. I suddenly remembered how much fun I used to have just making up stories and singing in my high school choir.

I used to attend a church called Remnant and I was asked to do a presentation for one of our women's nights. I was not sure what to do, so I decided to write a skit. I was not sure if this was a good idea or a bad one, but it was the first idea that came to mind. I wrote the script, asked some friends from work and other churches to help me, and pulled it off. It was the best feeling ever; that was my **"This Is It!"** moment. I received a lot of compliments from the women in the group, expressing how it helped them, made them laugh, and how much they enjoyed it. This was a defining moment because, during the process of writing and rehearsing, I had so much fun. The volunteers had fun. And the women at church enjoyed the production.

For me, this was a discovery. This meant I needed to change careers, network with new people, and pursue what I really wanted to be—an entrepreneur. My discovery led me towards a whole new path.

Goodbye, Corporate World! No more clocking in and out. No more monitored breaks and lunches. No more performance reviews. No more boring days and terrible bosses. And, most importantly, no more building someone else's company. I needed to start building my own. I had to let go of everything that was familiar. Having a corporate job meant a steady paycheck, consistency, and reassurance—until it didn't when I was laid off. I understood that the transition from the corporate world to full-time entrepreneur would not be easy. It would take time. But at least I had discovered what my desires were telling me.

Enlightened

I finally understood what was missing and why I was so dissatisfied. I had built a life based on providing and surviving, not a life full of passion or adventure. Before starting college, I remember telling someone who influenced me deeply that I wanted to be a writer. The response I received was that a writing career did not provide health insurance. From that point on, the decisions I made were "**Safe Decisions**" — decisions that allowed me to provide, pay bills, buy food, and get by. I was thriving externally, but miserable inside. I graduated with a degree that I was not interested in. Initially, I did not want to go to college; I wanted to take some time off and figure out what I wanted to do. But I went to college anyway because my mother insisted. I worked 8:00 a.m. to 4:30 p.m. jobs, worked overtime, arrived early, and stayed late.

These are things I was taught to do. What have you been taught? What do you believe that conflicts with your discovery? What are you doing right now that you wish you could quit doing tomorrow so that you could start doing something else? Once you unlearn certain patterns and become enlightened by what God is trying to show you, then everything will change.

Chapter 2: Discovery

1. Describe an event that happened to you or something that was said to you that has shaped your thought patterns.

2. How has your thought pattern affected the choices you have been making?

3. What "Safe Decision" are you making right now?

4. Describe how you have been enlightened.

Don't Tell Everybody

During your discovery, be careful who you talk to and share your desires and discovery with. If they are not a person with real faith, goals, and a plan for their own lives, then don't ask for or take their advice. Some people will not be able to see beyond your situation and will provide advice based on **"Safe Decisions."** If you can find people who have been all over the world, who have taken risks to build their dreams, who are not afraid of change, and who have changed their lives, ask them questions. Learn about their process and how they did it. This will give you insight and wisdom.

What About the Children?

I believe your children are the most important reason why you must discover the root of your desires and reprogram your mind. Children are not like adults. They have an innocence that causes them to believe in the things that adults deem impossible. Your children have desires, and, as they grow, those desires will develop into their gifts. If you are their primary example, they need to see your discovery of yourself. Your children need to see you lead by example.

Talk to your children, no matter their age, and ask them questions about their passions and what they would like to do. Based on their answers and your insight as a mom, ask yourself if your lifestyle enhances your children's lives in every way? Think about your physical location, your career, or your environment. Can they have better opportunities somewhere else? What type of training or education will they need for their passions? What kind of groups do they need to be a part of? Do you want them to be more cultured, to have access to more activities?

It is your job as a parent to help your child cultivate their gifts and talents. Financially providing for your children will always be your number one goal, and it should be. But, there is more than one way to do that. Once you discover what you really need to do then you can discover ways to have multiple streams of income or find the right path that will provide the level of income you desire.

After you have talked to your children answer the questions below for each of them.

Chapter 2: Discovery

Name: _____

1. What is their personality like?

2. What is their passion?

3. Where can these opportunities be found?

4. What activities are needed to enhance growth in this area?

5. What kind of life do you want them to have?

Chapter 2: Discovery

My Son

From a young age, I knew that my son would love music in some way, shape, or form. Before the age of three, he had a keyboard and a drum set, and he was banging on pots and pans. I thought for sure he would be a musician. But, after watching him more closely, I noticed when the music would start, he would start dancing. It did not matter where we were—the grocery store, taking a walk, riding in the car, or watching a movie. When the music started, so did he.

When he was about six years old, I realized that he was really good. At every church we went to, the Sunday school teachers would tell me how he just danced and danced, and how it inspired the other children to be more active during praise and worship. And then, of course, there were some teachers who did not agree with his style of dancing. He was break-dancing, pop-locking, flipping, and pulling off all kinds of kicks. This was who he was. I had to ask myself, *"Can my son develop his love for dancing in a small city?"* The answer was, "No. Too many limited opportunities." He would have never been able to express himself through the art of dancing without someone trying to get him to conform in a way that made them feel comfortable. Also, being a single mom and working full-time and long hours, I would not have been able to take him to classes or travel to competitions. Sometimes, I was just mentally drained.

My son is my forever. This means that, until he turns eighteen or until he is able to take care of himself after eighteen, I needed to be able to help him find his path. I could not do that if I did not follow my own.

Chapter 3

Decision

The decision to walk towards your path and find more is, first, mental, and then becomes a physical action. Take some time to renew and prepare your mind. The Bible says this is necessary.

> **"Do not conform to the pattern of this world but be transformed by the renewing of your mind"** (Romans 12:2).

This lets us know that our thought patterns are significant. Remind yourself multiple times a day of your desires and your discovery. This will be the new foundation for your life. You will be tempted to hang on to your old way of thinking. But you must have an active determination to **Never Give Up**!

Making a life-changing decision can bring on a whirlwind of emotions and questions. The most common question is: **How will I do this?** A lot of single moms allow this question to keep them stuck and unable to make decisions because all they see are the roadblocks. Roadblocks include not having enough money, not being able to take time off work, an unreliable car, bills being too high, not having enough hours in the day, bad credit, too many kids, no support system, and fear. There are many reasons that can put the decision on hold. **Faith is your** *how*. You must be mentally okay with not having all the answers up front. It may be necessary to get a coach, mentor, or spiritual leader who will truly invest in you. Sometimes, no matter how hard you try, you will not be able to do everything alone. This

Chapter 3: Decision

journey ain't no joke. You were never meant to do it alone.

1. Do you have a decision that you need to make? If so, what is that decision?

2. What roadblocks are stopping you from making decisions?

3. With faith, what can you do to get around these roadblocks?

4. List some coaches, mentors or spiritual leaders that can help lead you in the right direction.

Looking Back, It Hurt Me More Than I Knew

You do not always see how your choices are affecting you until you look back. You are then able to see the big picture, but, by then, it is often too late. Too much time passed. Too many missed opportunities. Too much time spent creating a life you did not really want. In the rearview mirror, you can clearly see all the things that happened that you did not really want to happen, actions that did not make any sense, and going in circles without making any real progress.

Fear and the "how" kept me stuck for most of my twenties. I suffered from a lot of regrets and years of my life that I can never get back. I made decisions based on other people's advice and suffered the consequences. I made decisions based on my own opinion and suffered the consequences. I was lost. I experienced high-stress levels, weight gain, high blood pressure, and depression. I was lonely, and I lost sight of who I was. I thought that I needed a therapist or medicine to improve my mental health. I talked to people who sincerely wanted to help, but they never did. It got to the point where making money wasn't enough, and I didn't even feel like a good mother because, at times, I was physically present but emotionally absent. I was drowning. No one could help me. Not being on the right path was costing me more than I realized. Finally, I could not take it anymore, so I made my decision.

Be honest with yourself about what is stopping you. You must be confident as you find your path. Confidence does not mean that everything will work out perfectly, but it does mean that you believe without a doubt that change is necessary. Once you begin to believe, God can show you a new perspective and new ways to accomplish your goals. Be patient with yourself.

Chapter 3: Decision

Transition is a journey that will be worth it in the end!

My Decision, My Path

First, I made a mental decision to move to Georgia, then I took action. Some people told me I should not move because I did not already have a job. Some said that because I am a single mom it wasn't wise to move away from close family. Someone also told me that, if it didn't work out, 'don't be prideful, just move back home.'

My son was struggling in school and had behavior problems at the time, so my mom wanted me to leave him with her in Indiana. She felt that I would not be able to keep a job if his behavior did not improve. She was my support system. She would leave work and pick him up from school if he was sick or misbehaving. I strongly considered leaving him with my mom for one year, so I could get settled. This was sound advice.

Chapter 3: Decision

Get Your Mind Right, It May Not Get Easier

When resigning from my job, I had people who I thought were friends trying to sabotage me, so I could not resign in good standing. If I did not resign in good standing, I would not get any paid vacation, which I needed, and I would not be re-hirable, ever. I had no intention of ever moving back, but I also knew that one could never know what could happen five or ten years down the road. In addition, if I ever found myself in a place where I wanted to be associated with this company, I would not be able to if I was not in good standing. I had all of this going through my mind, all of these reasons that suggested that I couldn't. This hit me hard.

That is why the decision is first mental. You may face a lot of opposition that may serve to convince you that having more is not possible. If no one else believed that there was more, I did. I had an advocate who was in management on the job that I resigned from, and I told her that, regardless of what happens, I was leaving. I did not do anything wrong, and that was my final decision. Moments later, I had another meeting with management, and things worked out in my favor. I resigned in good standing and received my paid vacation. But what if I had not fought for what I believed? What if I let the idea of not having that extra money stop me?

No matter what, I knew, regardless of what was going on around me, that I wanted more. Once I made the decision, action followed. I decided to take my son with me because I could not leave him behind and I wanted him to have a new start as well. My mom understood. No matter what advice I was given, I had to follow God's leadership in following through with my decision. This is why faith is so important:

God will not show everyone what he is showing you.

You may feel a lot of pressure from all the advice, and all the do's and don'ts but let it just be that — advice.

They Might Support You, They Might Not

It is only natural to want people to support you and validate your decisions, especially when you are raising kids alone and when you have so many responsibilities. Figuring things out can be a heavy burden and having a support system when you are making a life-changing decision makes the burden feel lighter. It is comforting. If you have that, count it a blessing. But if you do not, and you get overwhelmed in the process because your mind is clouded by the excitement and the task at hand, take some time and slow down. You may still have to work (maybe more than one job), take your kids to practice, help with homework, cook dinner, clean up, and do the laundry. Those tasks do not go away. But you can do this. Set small goals and do a little at a time.

When you experience moments where it feels like it's too much, talk to yourself about all the things that are going to happen for you. Give praise to God because you are not alone. Things are working out for you even though you do not see it. Be thankful in advance for the people he is putting in your life to help you along the way. Out of all the people I talked to about wanting to move and finding more, I can count on one hand the number of people who believed in me and my dreams. Shout-out to my mom and my best friends, Jasmine Lewis and Tracy Martinez—all who were single moms who helped when I made my decision.

I Decided and Leaped

Once my decision was made, I began actively preparing for my new path. I saved my money and sold my furniture. I had about $3,000.00. I rented a big SUV, put our stuff in totes, and hit the road. I moved away from Indiana.

I had spent years trying to find the courage to do it. I always used "good planning" as an excuse. I needed to wait until after tax season. I needed to wait six months and save. My son needed to finish elementary. So many excuses.

The moment I realized that I was not afraid, I stopped overthinking and made it happen. When I left with my son, I did not have a real plan regarding my career or finding a job. I just remember driving down the highway feeling relieved and excited, with no idea what was going to happen next. My brother-in-law and sister, Adoniss and Brittany, lived in Georgia and allowed us to stay in their home. I appreciate their love and support. I had to make the decision by myself. Once I arrived, I had help. God will make a way; you just have to decide to move forward.

Chapter 3: Decision

1. What resources do you need to start taking action?

2. What can you be doing now to make your transition easier?

3. How much time do you really need to accomplish your goals?

4. Based on your timeframe, write out a strategic plan to accomplish the goals needed to move forward.

What About the Children?

As a single mom, I encourage you to pray for wisdom. Your decision will affect your children. Depending on your path, your children will need time to transition as well. They may not understand what is best for them or what they need. Communicate with them, share what you have discovered, and share your excitement about what God has shown you. This does not guarantee that they will accept the new changes, but, as a family, you must communicate and work through it together. Never forget that your children have thoughts and feelings that should not be dismissed.

I moved away from my mom (and my son loves his Maw Maw). My son moved away from his friends and other family members. These situations are not the same for everyone. Although my son loves my mom, at the time he struggled so much, that I had no choice but to make a hard decision. From preschool through first grade, I could see that he was emotionally burdened and acting out. His grades suffered, he struggled to make friends, and he was not confident in himself. The school counselor called me at work almost every day with concerns about his mental health. He was in the first grade when he started talking about self-harm. His behavior issues went on for about three-and-a-half years. A few factors played into this: every teacher is not for every student and neither is every school. The school system is not always right. There isn't just one way to teach and discipline students.

My son asked me often why I wasn't married and compared our family to other families with both parents in the home. He would tell me he wanted a stepdad. I began to understand that although he is only a child, he recognized he did not have a complete family. He compared himself to other kids and believed they were better than him. He was telling me what was wrong through his behavior and conversation. My son had a good home life and a lot of great people who loved him and supported him during that time. But he did not know how to emotionally handle the other factors that were hurting him. That has been one of the hardest parts, seeing my son hurting internally and not being able to fix it. Therefore, my decision wasn't just for me it was for him too.

It can be easy to just label kids in a negative way, or discipline them when they are acting out, but that is not the answer. Mothers listen to what your children are saying and answer their questions. Sometimes our choices are affecting them. And sometimes situations happen that we have no control over. But children still bare the burden.

Chapter 3: Decision

1. Describe any struggles you see your children having.

2. What is the cause of these struggles?

3. What decision can you make that will help your children have a better mental, emotional, physical, and social life?

4. How can you create more effective ways to communicate with your children?

Chapter 3: Decision

A Whole Lot Changed, and Some Things Stayed the Same

A year after we left, I can tell you that everything worked out. My son loves school now. He had the best teacher named Mrs. Peltier who helped him transition and who accepted him and his dance moves. She saw his strengths and weakness and took time to learn how to teach him. I pulled her aside to ask how he was doing because I had not received one phone call from the school. I was not used to the silence. I experienced anxiety because I was not sure how he would transition. I described the behavior issues he had at school in Indiana and she said, "I do not know the kid you just described." He was one of the top students in her class. His grades were amazing. As a parent, I realized that certain environments do affect children.

Chapter 3: Decision

We found a dance academy, Rockwell Dance Academy, a dream come true for my son. They have great instructors and a community of parents and kids who support this form of art. He found where he belongs, and he is finding himself. He won first place in a national championship and he is happy. My decision to move gave my son something that overshadowed what made him sad. It gave him a life that he can look forward to living.

We still have our challenges though. We both miss my mom. My son still deals with trying to make new friends, missing home, and being in a new place. The memories of how life used to be do not go away. I found a job making good money, then I was laid off eight months later. There are a lot of moments where I do not know what to do next.

I get frustrated. I cry about things. Yes, I am still single, and still raising my son alone.

But, through all of that, I have no regrets about my decision. I have met so many people who have embraced us. They care about my goals and we are both in the right environment for endless possibilities.

I am no longer limited.

Every day, I am discovering new pieces of my path.

Chapter 4
What We Want

We all want more for our lives. Faith and belief must precede *more.* Without faith and belief, you will not embrace your desires, discover what's inside, or make a decision to move forward. When you first believe, God opens your heart and mind. He can't show you something you don't believe you can see. So, open up and listen to your inner voice! God wants you to have more for your life.

Every successful woman has found strength in her identity. There is no greater gift than finding the woman you really are. Your children are better when you have confidence and peace within. The right path will set you and your children up for success. Every step counts and the mistakes made while on your path are only lessons that you will use later on. Being a single mom will always have its challenges. Finding your path will not change the ups and downs of parenting. But it will give you boldness as a woman, knowing that you are headed in the right direction.

I was just a single mom, working, providing, and mentally struggling. Now, I am a woman with a purpose who raises her son to see life from a perspective full of possibilities. Anything is possible. I am a self-published author. I am a writer, a producer, and a director for the reality TV show *The Business Women of Atlanta*. I am also a songwriter who thrives on creativity.

These are just the beginning pieces to my puzzle which will unfold as I walk on my path. I still have more questions than answers, so faith leads my desires. I know who I am, and I am still learning to listen to my desires, so I can discover what I do not understand. And I will keep deciding that me and my son **are worth it.**

Chapter 5

From My Heart to Yours

Principles to Live By

Let me talk on a more personal level. You may find the courage to make a decision, but without the principles listed below you won't get far. We all want to be successful. Being a woman of good character is essential. People will honor good character, responsibility, and a good attitude over any everything else. If you do not learn these lessons, your life can be harder than what it needs to be. My life experiences have taught me these principles, some I've picked up from other people, and others I've developed myself. Many people find their path and success and then ruin it. If you can conquer yourself, then you can conquer the world.

Let's Begin!

- ❖ Do the right thing. It does not matter what anyone else does.

- ❖ If you are resigning from a job, put in your two weeks' notice, and leave in good standing if possible. A good work history and work reputation will benefit you.

- ❖ If you live with someone or are moving out of a location, clean up after yourself and your children and pay any outstanding balances. Landlords and leasing companies do background checks and check references. Leaving a property messy could have a negative effect when trying to move forward.

- ❖ Show up to work on time. Do a good job. If you don't like your job, still do your best.

- ❖ It is not okay to show up late everywhere you go. Have the spirit of excellence.

- ❖ Plan ahead if you know you have somewhere to be, pick out clothes for everyone and prepare meals the night before.

- ❖ It is always good to take snacks wherever you go; kids are always hungry.

- ❖ You must know yourself. The more you know about you, the easier it is to avoid pitfalls.

- ❖ Forgive yourself! What's done is done. Start learning ways to make things better instead of focusing on what went wrong.

❖ No one owes you anything, no matter how many kids you have. But, people will be more willing to help you if you have a grateful attitude and are appreciative.

❖ Do not panic when something goes wrong. Panicking can lead to irrational decisions.

❖ THINK before you react. Examine the situation and see beyond your emotions. React with a clear mind. Negative reactions can have heavy consequences.

❖ Your children will be children, so let them.

❖ Your children may not always understand how hard you work, but they will thank you for it later.

- Be an active parent at the school. Communicate with the teachers and principals. Be an advocate for your child.

- By the grace of God, you will always have your children, so take time to raise them.

- There is nothing easy about this, but I promise you, there will be much joy and confidence the more you accomplish.

- You are stronger than you know!

- A good credit score matters!

- Pay people back when you borrow from them. A long-lasting relationship is worth more than anything materialistic.

- You are not always right. Don't be afraid to apologize and admit when you are wrong.

❖ People will not always do what you want or do things the way you think they should.

❖ Follow your instincts. They are telling you what you haven't seen yet.

❖ When someone who loves you tells you that you are wrong, don't get mad. First, remember that they love you, then consider what they have said.

❖ Sometimes, only you will know the truth of a matter.

❖ Don't argue with people who have not walked in your shoes.

❖ Learn to be quiet! Silence can speak louder than words.

❖ You cannot change anyone.

❖ You are worth it. If no one else believes it, you need to.

- ❖ Teach people how to treat you.

- ❖ Laugh more! Learn to find humor in everything.

- ❖ How you feel matters.

- ❖ If you find yourself exhausted trying to defend yourself, just stop! People will think and do what they want!

- ❖ Pick your battles. Everything does not need to be a debate or argument. Be content just knowing you are right.

- ❖ You may never get an apology. Some people who do you wrong may never even look back to see if you are okay. Those people were never meant to be in your life anyway.

- ❖ Dysfunction is not okay. Don't get comfortable saying 'that's just me' when you have negative patterns. If you refuse to expand and grow, you will miss out on opportunities.

- Not all men are bad men. You just picked some bad ones.

- It's okay to let people with good intentions help you.

- If someone critiques you as a mother, learn from sound advice. You don't know everything.

- Do not compete against other women; there is no one else like you.

- One of the most important things to learn is how to build and maintain relationships. You will need people along the way.

- You might have to do things you don't want to do. Do them anyway.

- Learn to budget and save money.

- Get a savings account.

- It's okay to treat yourself to nice things.

- ❖ No, you don't have to be ashamed of being on public assistance; it's only temporary.

- ❖ Don't settle for a man who doesn't encourage and support your growth.

- ❖ Pray for wisdom and knowledge because there may be times when no one has the answers you need.

- ❖ It might not be fair; you might get overlooked. Keep going!

- ❖ It's okay to not want to talk to your kids all the time because you desire conversations with grownups.

- ❖ Loneliness is hard. Doing the right thing and growing as a woman sometimes means being alone.

- ❖ Invest in books, coaches, and products that inspire you. Your thoughts can be overwhelming, so it's important to have positive reinforcement.

Chapter 5: From My Heart to Yours

- ❖ Be willing to change your perspective. The way you view the world will determine how successful you can be.
- ❖ Change is uncomfortable.
- ❖ Decide the type of woman you want to be and work towards becoming her.
- ❖ Stop pretending. Be you; you will be happier.
- ❖ Some days you might feel beautiful; some days you might not. You are beautiful.
- ❖ Do what you know, not what you feel. Feelings are tricky and can be misguided.
- ❖ Some days you don't like your kids… I get it!
- ❖ There are no perfect moms. You will make mistakes.

- Some days you just want to be lazy and not even try. That's normal.
- Retail therapy will not solve your problems.
- Preparation is a key to success.
- Success looks different for everyone.
- Talk some sense into yourself when you need to.
- Yes, it is easier said than done. But it's not impossible.

Chapter 6

Self-Examination

Being a Single Mom

I could name all the negative stigma about single moms, especially if you have children by more than one father. But what good would that do? Everyone does not share the same belief system and, more importantly, it only matters what you believe about yourself. There are many successful single moms. I believe our success is because we do not see ourselves as just "single moms." We do not just see our struggles, our mistakes, or the current situation. We see where we are going, and never stop believing that we can get there.

Chapter 6: Self-Examination

1. What do you think about yourself? (Write down your honest thoughts.)

2. What is something positive someone has said to you as a single mom? How did those words make you feel?

3. What do you think about single moms as a whole?

4. Reflect on your thoughts. Are they more positive or negative? Make a list of all your positive attributes.

Triggers

Identify and gain control of your triggers. Triggers are words or actions by others that are taken personally. These words or actions make you feel targeted by others and result in a reaction such as going off. Learn your triggers and take time to understand why they bother you. Avoid situations that cause them and keep control over them. Be aware of them. Mastering what you are most sensitive about will make you stronger. If you do not master these triggers, your behavior will become a reflection of you, not the person or situation that caused it.

Chapter 6: Self-Examination

1. What are your triggers?

2. How do you feel after you have allowed someone's actions to cause a negative reaction?

3. List the people who usually trigger you by their words or actions.

4. How can you avoid these situations?

Note: People who think they know you, but really don't, can be the main ones who set off your triggers. Learn to politely say, "I do not want to discuss this with you," or "I do not like your behavior; we need to stay away from each other." Or you can just ignore them completely. You do not owe them your time or an explanation.

Expectations

One of the hardest lessons to learn with friends, family, others or your child's father is getting over expectations of how someone should respond to how you feel. When you do not get the response, you want or feel you deserve, intense sadness, anger, or rage can fester inside you. You may be right and have valid points-but when a conversation does not go as you feel it should-learn to let it go and walk away. No two people share the same mind or experiences, so people will not process or understand situations the same way. You will get exhausted trying to prove your point, so stop! Yes, it might be unfair, and you might have to bear the load. If so, learn to bounce back quickly and keep going.

Bouncing back quickly allows you to remain in control. It is beneficial to you because it teaches you not to let anyone take away your sanity or peace of mind.

1. Does hanging on to sadness, anger, or rage help your life?

2. How can letting go help your life?

Chapter 7
Your Love Life

It is only natural to want a whole family. Not just to have someone help you raise your kids, but because as a woman, you want to be loved. I do not believe God created families to be broken, but it happens. I do believe that he gives us the ability to start over. There are many reasons why a woman may be a single mom, the death of a partner/spouse, divorce, or the relationship did not work out. It is ok to want love and a complete family. But how you go about it, will make all the difference.

People might say a lot of things to you about finding love. I suggest you listen to people who can give sound advice, provide solutions that will enhance your mental growth, provide a different perspective, and teach you problem-solving skills. Please only share your thoughts and feelings with people who truly care about your desire to find love. It's essential to know what you want.

1. Do you still believe in love? If the answer is Yes or No, please explain why or why not.

2. What type of love life are you looking for?

3. What type of man do you want?

Chapter 7: Your Love Life

4. What good advice have you been given about finding love? Did you listen to this advice?

5. List the people in your life who you can share your thoughts and feelings with about your desire for love.

6. Are you mentally and emotionally ready to build a healthy relationship?

7. If not, what do you need to work on?

Chapter 7: Your Love Life

8. Are you currently in a relationship that you want to get out of?

9. What are your long-term goals for a healthy relationship?

Chapter 7: Your Love Life

Yes, A Man Will Love You and Your Children

The important thing about faith is that you must believe before it even happens. I have a very close friend who has three kids by two different fathers and she is now married. Her husband loves her and her kids. They now have a child together, so she has children by three different men. I asked her husband if he had concerns about the number of children she had. He said, "No, she has so much confidence. She takes care of herself and her children. I admire that about her." Let go of pre-conceived ideas about what a man might think of you.

Do not take it personally if a man does not want to walk into a situation with a woman who already has children. Everyone has a right to their own personal preference. You would never want to force anything. Never compromise yourself or your children just to be able to say, "I have a man," when there is someone out there willing to give you the world.

Be careful what type of men you let into your life and your children's lives. Just because a man accepts the fact that you have children does not mean he is a good fit. One thing I learned from observing my friend's situation is that a man must *want* a family. This must be valuable to him. A man provides for and protects what he values. You will know the difference between a man who loves you and your kids and a man who accepts it but does not make the effort to be a partner who helps you raise your kids. Remember, the person you allow into your children's lives becomes their example.

Chapter 8
Words Have Power.
Words of Affirmation.

Your words have power. Be careful what you say about yourself and others. As I previously mentioned, I hit a real low in my life at one point, and there was a time when I could not even pray. The words would not come out of my mouth. Every morning, my mom would turn on TBN, and Andrew Womack, Joyce Meyers, and Joel Osteen would play on every television in the house. At the time, I did not have much faith, but I listened because it was playing. I remember wishing I could find the words to say to God. So, when Joel Osteen came on, I figured that

Chapter 8: Words Have Power. Words of Affirmation.

if I couldn't find my own words and to avoid speaking negativity, then I would repeat his. I told myself that I was happy, courageous, strong, powerful, special, etc. Everything positive that came out his mouth, I said. Even though I did not believe it, I wanted to. It was like physical therapy. When you first start treatment, you might not start feeling better right away, and you might not see anything happening, but it is. I did this for years. Now, I refuse to say things that do not build me up.

If you do not have cable TV or the internet, go to a library or public place with WiFi and listen to inspirational messages over and over. Buy CDs and DVDs to listen to on repeat. Search YouTube, I do this often. My drive to work was about forty minutes long, and every morning, I listened to motivational speakers whom I found to be relatable. Yes, I talked to myself in the car. I do it so much now that, when a negative thought comes to my mind, I say:

Chapter 8: Words Have Power. Words of Affirmation.

I am confident.

I am secure.

I am brilliant.

I am talented.

I have the best ideas.

I am creative.

I get the best deals and contracts.

People want to buy my ideas.

I am a multimillionaire.

No one can do what I can do.

I am funny.

I am beautiful.

Chapter 8: Words Have Power. Words of Affirmation.

I am kind and full of compassion.

I am happily married to a kind and compassionate man.

He is handsome. He is mentally, physically, and emotionally healthy. He is wealthy. We are the best of friends, and he is a good father to our son.

This is what I see for myself. This is what I CHOOSE to believe. This is what I say to myself when doubt begins to cloud my mind. The more you speak affirmations to yourself, you will have great thoughts about yourself, your life, and what you want out of it. Better than that, you will believe it!

Chapter 8: Words Have Power. Words of Affirmation.

Words of Encouragement to Single Moms from Supporters All Around the World.

Life happens. You got this.

Continue to dream and make your dreams come true.
Doris H. "Granny"

Trust God and He will make your ways prosperous.

Reach for the stars and beyond.

Listen and grow with your children; they will be a blessing to you.
Ms. Brenda H.

You are an amazing mom. You are doing a great job!
Isaiah C.

Don't stress about doing everything. Just take one step at a time.

Chapter 8: Words Have Power. Words of Affirmation.

> Victoriah G.

It's hard, but you can do it. Step back and look how far you have come.
> Gail H.

Embrace your singleness. You can enjoy life during every cycle.
> Linda D.

It's never too late to be all you can be.
> Tyra H.

Nothing is too hard for God. He will direct your path.
> Dominic F.

Life is too short. Take time to enjoy yourself!
> Winford & Debra J.

Children are a blessing from God. Love, cherish and take care of us.
> Karter and Kaelyn G.

Chapter 8: Words Have Power. Words of Affirmation.

Love your children and they will return the love.

Dorothy H.

Take care of yourself. Learn to laugh and have a lot of fun.

Melvin & Faye D.

Teach your children to love God. They will make you proud.

Hattie D.

You can do all things through Christ. Trust, believe, and keep the faith.

Joey & Tameka H.

I am a single dad. When my daughter tells me she needs me, I wonder does she know I need her more.

Michael G.

Mothers are very influential in a child's life. Stay strong, stay encouraged; we need you.

Kimberly Warren

Chapter 8: Words Have Power. Words of Affirmation.

With God, all things are possible. Continue to let your light shine.

Don't give excuses as to why you can't accomplish your goals or succeed in life. Work hard, push through it and succeed.
Adoniss & Brittany Gibson

You and your children are worthy of true love. Never let anyone convince you that you are not. Not even yourself.
Samuel & Jasmine Lewis

You are not a single mom. You are raising your child in a single parent home. Adjust your mindset. Talk to yourself as if God can hear you!
Angela Sims

Chapter 8: Words Have Power. Words of Affirmation.

You are an unstoppable, beautiful, creative force! Your children are some of your most amazing creations, but don't stop there- continue to be creative in your life, your family, and your business!

#KeepCreating

Michel C.

A Special Thank You to My Book Supporters

Angela Sims, Tracy Martinez, Theresa Johnson, Walter & June Gordon, Edwin & Rosalyn Butts, Adoniss & Brittany Gibson, Bradley Gardner, Samuel & Jasmine Lewis, Quynh Bui, Kimberly Warren, Jameeka Montgomery, Rachel Genese Potter, Dominic Fletcher, Wendy Ward, Lavinia Marshall, Thomas & Zalima Alexander-Williams, Dr. Tyra Wingo, Jacqueline Waddy, Doris H, Ms. Brenda H, Isaiah C, Victoriah G, Gail H, Linda D, Tyra H, Winford & Debra J, Karter G. Kaelynn G, Dorothy H, Melvin & Faye D, Hattie D, Charlene S, Regina A, Corry S, Darla G, Donna S, Cortney C, Evans Family, Joey & Tameka H.,

Reginald & Lillie Smith
RNL Meals
Facebook & Instagram: RNL Meals

Tia Boyer
The Imagery Artistry, Inc
Theimageartistry@gmail.com
Facebook: Tia's Imagery Artistry

Dr. Michel Cockerham
Jade Link Consulting
Facebook: Jade Link Consulting

I would like to extend a special thank you to my spiritual and life coaches, Angela Sims and Lavinia Marshall. Thank you for your support, your mentorship, and for believing in me.

Lavinia Marshall / Totally You
Laviniamarshall.com
Facebook & Instagram: Lavinia Marshall
Twitter: @SpeakLavinia

Angela Sims / League of Girlfriends
Facebook & LinkedIn: Angela Sims
Twitter & Instagram: @ACJSims

About the Author

Sharita is an author and an entrepreneur. She decided to rewrite her story and did. She is determined to use her experiences and her faith to motivate, inspire, and encourage everyone she meets. She leads by example to show others that anything is possible and to never give up. Sharita is an advocate for single moms and is determined to teach them to not be afraid of transition.

Sharita's new career path has led her to be able to write, direct, and produce a reality TV show *The Business Women of Atlanta*, and to write songs, plays, and scripts for feature films. She has discovered her passion. This is only the beginning. The story is still being written.

Follow Sharita on Social Media

Sharita Latham
The Business Women of Atlanta

@Ritarenee27
The Business Women of Atlanta

www.ingramcontent.com/pod-product-compliance
Lightning Source LLC
Chambersburg PA
CBHW070528100426
42743CB00010B/1990